AF526681

Contract Drafting Tips & Tricks

Contract Drafting
Tips & Tricks

Bhumesh Verma
Advocate

OakBridge

Published by
OakBridge Publishing Pvt. Ltd.
M 35, 1st Floor, Old DLF, Gurugram, 122001, Haryana, India
Tel.: +91 124 4305970, E-mail: info@oakbridge.in
www.oakbridge.in

ISBN: 978-93-95764-17-9

Printed and bound at Saurabh Printers Pvt. Ltd.

Drafting and interpreting commercial contract goes to the root of drafting and advocacy skills. There are several niceties which needs to be kept in mind. Bhumesh's tips on commercial contracts drafting provide practical insights to students and professionals alike.

—Dr. Vijay Kumar Singh,
Professor and Dean,
Faculty of Law SRM University,
Delhi-NCR Sonipat

This book is just like a daily mandatory potion on contract drafting and the compilation by Bhumesh is well articulated and wonderfully knitted to provide hands-on to the essentials of contract drafting.

—Dr. Deevanshu Shrivastava, Head,
Faculty of Law,
Jagran Lakecity University, Bhopal

Short, crisp and beneficial tips on Drafting of commercial contracts - a quick guide to effective and practical structuring of commercial contracts.

—Dr Deepa Shrivastava, Senior Assistant Professor,
Department of Law PIMR, Indore

Bhumesh's extraordinary experience as a legal practitioner and his penchant for teaching always result in writings power packed with practical insights and yet are easy to understand. This book is a testament to these two rare gifts.

—Tanuj Kalia, CEO Lawctopus

Bhumesh has inspired a generation of young lawyers to draft better contracts through his lectures and sharing daily tips to improve their drafting skills. It's amazing that he has now put the tips together in one place. This would be very valuable for law students and young lawyers.

—Ramanuj Mukherjee, CEO Lawsikho

Contracts are an inseparable part of our lives. The tips in the book are crisp, clear and insightful, delving deep into the intricacies of contract drafting. An absolute must-have.

—Ami Jain – Advocate, Mumbai

Bhumesh is an expert in contract drafting and his daily tips on contract law since last couple of years reflect his passion and dedication to share his knowledge. I have immensely benefited by reading his immensely valuable daily tips and am sure this his decision to print such tips in the form of a book will benefit everyone dealing with contracts.

—Srirama Murthy, Advocate, Hyderabad

Bhumesh has been posting excellent practical tips on contract drafting on daily basis. I am sure this book will be very useful to government departments, law firms, lawyers, academicians, law students, In-house Counsel, business community and other professionals.

—Jaydeep Mehta, Designated Partner,
Lexstreet Advisors LLP

There could have been no better legal expert and specialist than Bhumesh Verma to render these useful tips, based on his invaluable experience, regarding operational aspects of commercial, corporate, and transactional laws. He is best known for creatively harmonising theoretical and practical facets of these branches of law.

—Hemant Batra,
Corporate-Commercial and
Public Policy Lawyer

Dear Readers,

Success is a journey, not a destination—Zig Zagler.

A lot of professionals and students keep asking me, "How can I be an expert in contract drafting?" or "What is a perfect draft contract?".

I have no answer. Our efforts and learning cannot stop at any age or stage. Every profession demands constant improvisation. Same goes with contract drafting; it is a craft and requires experiential learning. One needs to keep learning, practicing, analysing and improvising.

Whatever little I know about contract drafting, I have been very happy to share with fellow professionals, academics, and students.

The focus of my legal practice, writings, teachings, and trainings in this domain has been to cultivate a culture of simple, understandable, commercially effective, and legally and enforceable contracts.

I have been sharing daily tips on contract drafting, encompassing several aspects, on social media for more than two years. These tips have received millions of views and innumerable validations, suggestions, and feedback from the fraternity.

In this book, we have collated some of the most interesting and important of these tips.

These tips should serve as preliminary guidelines for you when drafting contracts in a way that optimises everyone's time and resources and ensures the safeguarding of your client's interests. These are my suggestions, and in no way do they constitute any legal opinion or advice.

My book, "Practical Guide to Drafting Commercial Contracts," already adorns the libraries and desks of law and management schools, professional firms, professionals, and students. This book aspires to be a companion to that book and should serve as a daily routine and ready reckoner on the art of contract drafting.

Thanks to the OakBridge team for bringing this book from the conceptual stage to its present form.

Happy reading and drafting.

Bhumesh Verma

Contents

Introduction

1. Never take contract drafting as a mechanical job – cut, copy, paste from a precedent and think your job is done.

2. A contract is as much a living thing as the people, business and economy it affects. My friend Nick Gould would say even contracts affect lives. Therefore, be conscious and respectful to each drafting assignment you get.

3. Your drafting should be such as if the reader is watching a movie or looking at a picture and can capture your writing in visual. The reader should be able to visualise the events, situations, interactions, meetings, etc., by reading the contract. If the reader does, you have done a great job.

4. Each client has different expectations, resources, mindset, leverage, negotiating power, long term/short term perspective and other aspect(s).

5. Pay adequate attention to these aspects and only then start drafting.

6. A Contract is not just a nominal written document meant to meet the client's specifications. Consider the contract as a speech you are preparing to deliver to an audience. What aspects will you take care of if you are to speak considering the prospective audience of your contract? Incorporate the same prudence in your writing.

Let us discuss what aspects we should take into consideration if we are to consider drafting akin to speaking.

KISS Principle

1. Keep the KISS principle in mind.

   Keep It Simple and Stupid

   or

   Keep It Short and Sweet

   or

   Keep It Short and Simple

2. Remember the contract may be drafted by lawyers but is required to be implemented by non-lawyers.
3. Therefore, keep everything so simple that anyone reading your contract can understand its contents and the intent of the parties.
4. A contract should not be like a doctor's prescription. Everyone reading it should be able to understand it as much as possible.
5. The bottom line is, keep the language of your contract as simple as possible.

What has been your experience with simplicity or otherwise in this context?

Choose Your Words Wisely

1. Be a miser with words. Treat words as your money. Write everything that is required in your contract, but without repetition. Same thing at different places may mean different things and a word or two missing here and there at different places can turn the contract and its enforceability upside down.

   You love Jalebis, don't you? Even I do. However, not in contract drafting.

2. Stop going round in circles, beating around the bush. Mostly, it happens when you are clueless and know less/nothing about the subject matter.

3. Carry a thorough research (legal and otherwise), and come straight to the point so that everyone can understand.

   In this jet age, no one has the time for a 'literary journey'. 'Action' is the key word.

4. The shortest distance between two points is a straight line.

   Write crisp.

5. Don't discard Jalebi concept altogether, retain the crisp writing, discard the round long winding expressions.

   Just like Jalebis, don't serve Khichdi to your clients in the garb of a contract.

   When a contract is drawn from several different templates, it ends up being a 'khichdi'* that does not have a consistent flow or style, seems disjointed at places and is not consistent or coherent, and even contradictory at some places.

*Apart from the popular dish name, we use the word 'Khichdi' to describe a thing that is an unbalanced mix of different things, a hodgepodge .

6. Even if you are relying on multiple templates, at the end of it, do ensure that your contract reads as one consistent statement.

7. Do not leave your brain elsewhere while drafting a contract. See if everything (yes, EVERYTHING) in the contract is logical and makes sense.

8. If you notice something which is weird, unusual or different from the market practice, it's time to recheck.

9. You will detect these flaws only if you read the complete contract. Do not cut, copy, paste mechanically.

10. Whatever does not make common sense, cannot make legal or business sense (mostly!).

"He puts a positive spin on everything."

Preparatory Work for Contract Drafting

1. Once you get a mandate for contract drafting, process all the information you have received from the client.
2. Prepare a checklist of the missing information.
3. Be resourceful. Out of the missing information, find out what is available in the public domain.

4. Send a requisition list to the client only for information you cannot access from anywhere.

5. Do not bother clients every now and then with queries. Consolidate as many queries as you can in your first message itself.

6. Know the client, understand the proposed business, know the market condition and prevalent customs, try to understand some technical terms pertaining to the business/ transaction.

Memorandum of Understanding (MOU)

1. There is a lot of confusion between an MOU and a contract/an agreement.

   An MOU is a contract. Correct.

   An MOU is not a contract. Correct.

2. The key lies in the contents/intent of the MOU and not the nomenclature.

3. Do not simply discard an MOU assuming that it is not a contract and thus not enforceable.

4. Before you start drafting a contract, collect all necessary information from the client, particularly if there has been any MOU/ Letter of Intent or the like. Incorporate and elaborate on the terms of this preliminary document and add the aspects missing therein.

5. Do not deviate from the terms of the MOU, unless it is illegal, defies common sense, witnesses change in the circumstances or parties' understanding or your client has advised you otherwise.

6. In business discussions, invariably an MOU is an 'Agreement to Agree', encapsulating the preliminary understanding reached between the parties to pursue a transaction. A comprehensive and detailed contract is to be executed within the timeline and is subject to fulfilment of conditions set forth in the

MOU. If the preconditions are not satisfied or the deadline expires, the MOU comes to an end.

7. Different shades of MOU

   a. Sometimes parties articulate their preliminary understanding on a proposed transaction in an MOU. Their relationship is only exploratory and if they cannot reach a definite understanding and execute a contract relating to the transaction within a specified time, the MOU lapses without any legal consequences to either party.

   b. Sometimes parties write down the summary of their basic understanding in the MOU, provide the timeline in the MOU for a comprehensive contract subject to several preconditions (negotiation, due diligence, approvals, etc.). If the preconditions are not met within the timeline, the MOU lapses. There are no legal consequences of the

MOU or its expiry, other than those specifically agreed to in the MOU.

c. If an MOU fulfils all requisite requirements for a valid contract, incorporates complete understanding of the parties on the subject matter in adequate detail and has legal enforcement provisions, it is a contract. The mere nomenclature will not impede its validity or enforcement.

Legal Enforceability of MOUs

1. If an MOU entails monetary transactions, e.g., an advance, part payment, reimbursement of expenses, etc. and the MOU lapses due to the contemplated transaction not working out, what would you do?

   Incorporate a mechanism for the recovery, refund, forfeiture, adjustment, etc. of this money in the MOU and make such clause(s) and specify it to be enforceable.

2. If you are sharing some vital, confidential information with a party pursuant to an MOU, you should insist on confidentiality thereof (irrespective of whether the proposed transaction works out or not). Breach of confidentiality should invite consequences; else no one will take it seriously.

3. Make confidentiality provisions legally enforceable even if other provisions of the MOU are not.

4. Parties to an MOU invariably insist on exclusivity of discussions on the subject matter till they decide whether to go with the contemplated transaction or not.

5. No party is supposed to discuss or negotiate the same subject matter with a third party, else it will become a bidding game. To make the other party serious about this obligation, make it legally enforceable – any violation should entail legal consequences.

6. If you want some or all the provisions of an MOU to be legally enforceable, incorporate a clause towards the end encapsulating such provisions. Else, your client may not have a legal recourse for any violation.
7. If no provisions are to be legally enforceable, the MOU cannot be equated to a contract.

Shades of MOU

1. Do not keep an MOU open ended, unless it is an enforceable contract in itself. If the MOU is only preliminary in nature and the parties intend to execute a comprehensive agreement at a later stage to initiate a commercial transaction, fix a validity period for the MOU.

2. Provide 'what happens on expiry/termination of the MOU' towards the end.

3. Do the parties have the flexibility to extend the validity period of the MOU?
4. Do the parties have the right to waive any preconditions laid in the MOU and move ahead with execution of a definitive agreement irrespective?
5. Do any legal obligations attach to the parties post the termination/expiry of the MOU?
6. Do any clauses survive?
7. When you draft a contract preceded by an MOU between the parties, stipulate that the contract incorporates the entire understanding between the parties and supersedes the MOU.

Just in case there is an issue!

"Just to get the negotiation off on the right foot,
I don't intend to concede anything."

Contract elements: Title

1. The title of a contract is very important. It is your job to assess the legal relationship of the parties and/or nature of the contemplated transaction(s) under the contract; give a suitable title accordingly. Don't merely go by the client's understanding or the title on the template.

2. If you have not been diligent about assigning a correct title to a contract and there is a

dispute between the parties as to the nature of their relationship or the transaction, the court or any other adjudicator will have to go beyond the title. You should, therefore, be careful from day 1 and name the contract appropriately.

After the title, describe the full name of the contract with the date and place of execution.

'This Technology Transfer Agreement is executed on 13 August, 2020 at New Delhi between:'

"Great plan. Could we get some more details?"

Parties to a Contract

1. Check who are the parties that (i) have a role to play in performing a contract; (ii) are beneficiaries under the contract; (iii) are confirming parties/guarantors, etc. Thereafter, decide on who are the parties to the contract. Sometimes, eligible parties are left out, raising issues of privity of contract while trying to enforce it, while sometimes, parties without a role are unnecessarily made to execute a contract.

2. Correct description and identification of the parties is important for the enforcement of a contract, whether for effecting payments, asserting your rights, sending legal notices or court summons, etc. Be particular, specific, and accurate.

3. In the description of the parties, mention the full official name of every party (as evidenced by a government issued ID or registration) and not abbreviated names, nicknames or incomplete names.

4. In the party's description, mention the residential address of individual parties evidenced by a government issued identification document.

5. In the description of parties which are corporate bodies or other entities, mention their registered/corporate or other office as evidenced by the concerned authorities' records (e g. MCA). Do not mention a director or officer's residential address merely because he finds it more convenient.

6. For individual parties, mention a permanent identification proof (e.g., PAN, Aadhar, etc.) in the description. Passport numbers keep changing on renewal.

7. For authenticating the identification of a party which is a corporate entity, indicate a permanent registration number, e.g., PAN, CIN or likewise, in its description.

8. In the description of the parties, define them by their name, abbreviation or their role under the contract. Never as 'First party', 'Second party' or 'Party of the first part', 'Party of the second part' and so on.

9. Check the legal competence of the parties (age, mental health, capability to comprehend, etc.). If you find anything to the contrary, suggest a legal way out.

10. While checking the legal competence of the parties, check if the charter documents, by-laws, etc. of an entity permit it to undertake the proposed transaction. Else, it could be held *ultra vires,* jeopardising other parties' position.

Place of Contract

1. If different parties are executing the contract at different places, indicate the 'Place with Parties' signature on the signature page. The contract should start without indicating the place of execution as mentioned below:

   'This Distributorship Agreement executed on 14th August, 2020 between:'

Date of Contract

1. If different parties are executing a contract on different dates, mention the execution date on the signature page against each party's signature (like place of execution in the previous tip).

2. If both the place and date of execution of a contract are different for the parties, take both these elements to the signature page and the contract may start like this:

   'This Franchise Agreement is executed between:'

Recitals or Background clause

1. *Inter alia* apprises the readers about the parties, their business background, prior discussions about the subject matter or the purpose/goal of the contract. It also constitutes parties' representation to each other.

2. Recitals are akin to a precursor to the operative part of the contract. The objective is to acquaint the reader with the parties and

their proposed transaction. In the absence of recitals, the reader may have to gauge the nature of a contract by its title and/or going through the entire contract.

3. Recitals, like a story, should be about the past, not about the future. It is like a narrator or a Sutradhaar.

   Therefore, there is no need to mention the provisions of operative and boilerplate clauses in the recitals, a sentence about the proposed transaction will do.

4. Do not go overboard with recitals. Write only as much is essential.

   Unnecessary and irrelevant details may put the reader off track and one may even lose the patience to go through the contract.

5. Ensure the recitals are factually correct as they constitute the representations of the parties (e.g., qualification, capacity, intent, ownership, etc.). You could be held responsible for any loose cannons in

the recitals. Tread with caution and check minutely.

6. Arrange the recital clauses in a chronological order for easy understanding.

7. The agreement clause follows the recitals whereby the parties provide their confirmation to the terms of the agreement.

8. Consider the following examples:

    a. Now, therefore, in consideration of the premises, mutual promises, payments, considerations and covenants contained in this agreement and other good and valuable considerations (the validity, receipt and adequacy of which are hereby mutually acknowledged), the parties agree as follows:

    b. This agreement witnesses as under:

    c. The parties agree as under:

9. You may write as simple or as complicated an agreement clause as you want.

10. Ultimately, it boils down to all the provisions in the agreement considered together. Consideration, promises, covenants, etc. aspects have to be captured in the operative and standard clauses of the agreement anyways – agreement would be incomplete without them.

11. Every clause of an agreement need not start with 'That'. Litigation lawyers trying their hand at contract drafting are pro at demonstrating 'That' in every clause.

12. I recommend provisions to be listed numerically instead of alphabetically or alphanumerically. The reason is alphabets exhaust after z and you have to think how to go thereafter, (aa), (za), (zaa) or (zza) or what.

13. Clauses can be broken up further with numbers like (1.1), (2.3.2), etc. It is much easier to comprehend.

Definition/ Interpretation Clauses

1. The substantive provisions of the contracts invariably start with 'Definitions' and/or 'Interpretation clauses'.

2. A definition is a statement of the meaning of a term (a word, phrase, or other set of symbols). Definitions can be classified into two large categories, definitions which try to give the sense of a term and definitions which try to list the objects that a term describes.

3. The most important reason for inserting definitions in a contract is the brevity they bring. A word or two can convey a lot, for example, 'Company' can be used to describe ________ Limited, a company incorporated under the Companies Act, 2014 having CIN ______ and its registered office at _________. Instead of this detailed description, one word can convey the same meaning throughout the contract.

4. Definitions are also important because they enable us to have a common and focused understanding of a term; they ensure all parties are on the same page when discussing or reviewing a particular term and there is no divergence in understanding or commitment. For example, if 'Net Revenue' is defined as 'Sales - (specific) expenses', it is clear between the parties and there is no divergence in the parties' understanding.

5. If your contract needs a considerable number of terms defined, Clause 1 should be the definition clause. Arrange definitions in alphabetical order, so that they are easy to locate.

6. Ensure that all the defined terms in the definitions clause are actually used in the contract, else you cut a sorry figure and it appears a poor cut and paste job. Sometimes, while revising the draft on your own or during negotiations, the provisions carrying a defined term may vanish completely, eliminating the need for the defined term.

7. You need to define a term only if it is used more than once in the Contract. Else, the term/concept can be easily explained in the relevant provision itself.

8. Preferably, define a term with first letter in upper case and the following ones in lower case, e.g., Company, Investor, etc. Do not define in all caps, as much as possible. A term like LANDLORD implies you are emphasising too much or even shouting.

   In fact, do not use all caps anywhere in the contract, as much as possible.

9. However, there is an exception to this.

You may define a term in all caps, if it is an acronym, abbreviation of a party, organisation, documents, places, business terminology, etc.

Some examples: SBI for State Bank of India, GOI for Government of India, TCS for Tata Consultancy Services, TAT for turnaround time, JVA for Joint Venture Agreement.

10. Define a term only once in a contract. Sometimes, we see a term defined more than once (in recitals, definition clause, operative/boilerplate clause, annexures, etc.). This could be due to oversight or copying and pasting provisions from different precedents. In all this, you may end up defining the same term differently at different places, causing ambiguity, sowing seeds for a dispute.

11. Sometimes, there could be a series of contracts in pursuance of a corporate/commercial transaction. A comprehensive agreement may contain definitions to be used in all the linked agreements. If that is so, mention the fact.

12. After the definitions clause, you may also add an 'Interpretation clause' for helping the readers as to how some terms should be interpreted if the reader is confused! For example, will 'he' include 'she' ?

13. Immediately after the definition/ interpretation clause, the next clause should mention the transaction(s) for which the contract is being executed, with adequate details and clarity.

14. I have seen some intelligent lawyers so engrossed in other provisions that they forget to mention the transaction in the body of the contract itself!

Operative Part of a Contract

1. The operative clauses of a contract are commonly understood and referred to as the 'body' of a contract. These clauses are peculiar, distinct and the salient features of a contract and incorporate the key terms and conditions governing respective rights and obligations of the parties.

2. Boilerplate clauses are also known as standard clauses, miscellaneous clauses or

general clauses. These clauses are invariably incorporated at the end of most contracts. These clauses guide parties as to how should they act in different situations and clarify the relationship between the parties.

3. Boilerplate clauses or standard terms and conditions are invariably considered secondary to the operative provisions due to their standard language and are mostly transposed from one agreement to another. They should not be mistaken as unimportant and I advise equal attention be paid to them as operative clauses. A misunderstanding (culminating into a dispute) can arise out of any provision.

4. In terms of their placement in a contract, most operative clauses are placed in the beginning and boilerplate clauses (or standard terms and conditions) are incorporated towards the end.

Operative Part of a Contract

1. The transaction clause must specify what each party is supposed to bring to the table (literally), i.e., its role under the contract. For example, if a party is to manufacture/ deliver some goods or services, you may enclose an annexure explaining the nature of such goods or services. The deliverables may be explained in one or more clauses and annexures as well, if need be.

2. Apart from the details of the transaction, consideration is the most important aspect of a contract. Legal definitions apart, consideration is the reason for parties to get into a contractual relationship. Consideration is parties' takeaway from a contract, different takeaways for different parties - it could be money, goods, services, promise to perform or abstain or something different.

   Consideration aspects too can be captured in one clause or more.

3. Clearly provide each party's deliverables under a contract. What goods, services, money, promise, etc. it is supposed to deliver to whom, when, where and how (in what form and through which means)?

4. Along with each party's deliverables under a contract, stipulate the expected/promised/agreed performance standards and timelines. Also mention the remedies for a breach if these parameters are not adhered to.

5. Mention the currency of transaction clearly if the parties are from different jurisdictions - in what currency shall the products/services be billed and paid for. This will avoid differences between the parties at a later stage on the subject.

6. Provide the basis of the calculation of consideration - say, unit of time or product or service. A fee/remuneration may be paid on an hourly, daily, weekly, monthly or yearly basis or per visit or inspection charges or per piece of a product. The basis of charge should be clear.

7. Incorporate a clear-cut billing process for goods/services - frequency, addressee of the invoice, timelines and mode for submission of invoice, payments terms, etc.

8. Specify what taxes are associated with the transaction and fix the parties' respective responsibility for levying, collecting, deposit and providing appropriate certification, particularly the withholding tax.

9. Specify the consequences of non-payment within the stipulated time - penalty, interest, stoppage of work, notice, termination, etc.

10. Wherever you are mentioning any numerical amounts (money or otherwise), write it in numbers followed by words for clarity and confirmation.

11. For example, INR 5,000 (Indian Rupees five thousand only), 500 (five hundred) tonnes of material, etc.

12. Any typographical error in numbers can be easily detected if mentioned both in numbers and words.

13. Whenever you incorporate an interest percentage, specify where it is per month or per annum. I have seen many contracts omitting this simple yet critical element resulting in issues.

Pre-conditions

1. If the parties need to fulfil certain preconditions to become eligible/competent to initiate the transaction contemplated under the contract, specify these preconditions. For example - deposit of advance, securing internal external approvals, submission of documents/reports, etc.

2. Stipulate a timeframe for the fulfilment of all the preconditions.

Invariably, a contract or transaction becomes effective only upon the fulfilment of all these preconditions - if there are any exceptions, mention that.

2. Fix the responsibility for fulfilling the preconditions - indicate which party is responsible for which action.

3. Incorporate the consequences of non-fulfilment of the preconditions. Do the parties call off the transaction completely, partially, extend the deadline for fulfilment or waive the preconditions to go ahead?

4. Be judicious to demarcate which preconditions can be waived, if not fulfilled.

   You cannot waive any condition if it is legally mandated for a transaction to go through, (e.g., an RBI/CCI/SEBI approval for the transaction), else you run the risk of your transaction being void and unenforceable.

OR
MAYBE?
DECISIONS:
YES
OR NO

Lock-in Period

1. Many contracts (e.g., leasing, investment agreements, etc.) have a lock-in provision. A lock-in signifies the minimum engagement period. The parties cannot walk out of the relationship before expiry of the lock-in period. The rationale behind a lock-in is that everyone wants to do business with serious parties committing to continue engagement for a long (or reasonable) time.

2. If a party terminates a contractual relationship within the lock-in period, it has to pay a consideration to the other party for the entire agreed upon lock-in period. For example, if a tenant terminates a lease after 6 months (out of an agreed lock-in period of 1 year), it is liable to pay rent for the remaining 6 months even without possessing or using the premises.

3. While drafting or negotiating a lock-in clause, observe which party are you representing, whether a lock-in is in the interest of your party or not, if it is good for your party, whether it should be a long or a short period. Propose or negotiate accordingly.

Confidentiality/ Non-Disclosure

1. During the course of negotiating or performing a contract, one or more parties share a lot of information with each other. To protect proprietary, vital, and important information from unauthorised dissemination, you must insist on a confidentiality clause. In some cases, even a separate, standalone confidentiality or non-disclosure agreement may be necessary.

'This Confidentiality and Non-Disclosure Agreement (the "Agreement") is entered into by and between ________ with its principal offices at ________ ("Disclosing Party") and ________, located at ________ ("Receiving Party") for the purpose of preventing the unauthorised disclosure of Confidential Information as defined below'

2. While drafting this clause the first thing that is required is to define 'Confidential Information'. Unless the disclosing party specifies and the recipient party is aware of what information should be treated with care, this clause is of no use. Define confidential information as clearly and exhaustively as appropriate.

3. Not only the inclusions, but you should also demarcate the exclusions from the definition of confidential information. For example, information that is in the public domain (MCA/SEBI websites, media reports, etc.) cannot be treated as confidential information.

4. Specify the purposes for which the confidential information can be used. Any deviation from this path should not be tolerated.

5. Limit the dissemination of confidential information only to employees/agents/advisors of the recipients who have a need to know that confidential information to perform/review the contract.

6. If a recipient is required to disclose the confidential information in some legal proceedings, etc., insist upon limiting the disclosure as much as possible and intimate the disclosing party about the requirement of such disclosure.

7. Provide remedies for the disclosing party if the recipient discloses the confidential information in violation of the agreed terms of the contract.

8. Provide a timeframe for confidentiality obligations – whether the recipient is to maintain the confidentiality of the

information only during the term of contract or does the obligation survive the termination or expiry of the contract.

9. Use 'Will' to indicate the future happenings/ conditions/consequences.

   Use 'Shall' to indicate an obligation to be fulfilled by one or more parties.

   Do not mix up the usage of 'Will' and 'Shall'.

Exclusivity Clause

1. See if the parties expect exclusivity of business dealings from each other in respect of some particular products, services, discussions, geographical area, etc.

2. If so, incorporate a suitable provision.

3. The reason behind an exclusivity clause is to imbibe commitment and seriousness among the parties to dedicate all their efforts

and resources towards the success of the subject project/contract and not indulge in two-timing.

4. Define the period of exclusivity, definitely during the term of the contract. In some cases, parties may also agree on a cooling off period after the expiry/termination of a contract within which they will not deal with other parties.

5. Invariably, an exclusivity clause is incorporated in an employment agreement, putting an employee under the obligation to work solely for the employer during the term of the employment contract.

6. An exclusivity clause can put parties under business/financial strain and make them lose out on alternative business opportunities. If your client is worried about such opportunities and does not want to commit to exclusivity, negotiate and draft accordingly (either eliminating or limiting the exclusivity aspect).

7. An exclusivity clause can be beneficial for your client in controlling who the other parties work with, to get a competitive advantage in the market and becoming a trendsetter.

8. In the absence of exclusivity, the other party may be offering similar goods or services to your client's competitors and its goods and services will become commoditised, losing their distinct commercial standing and brand equity.

9. If your client is asked to commit to exclusivity, you should bargain for a significant volume of business and a long duration of contract. Committing exclusivity for a small volume or duration does not make sense.

10. Ensure that your exclusivity clause is not hit by 'Restraint of Trade' aspect.

11. Ensure that your exclusivity clause makes common sense, sounds reasonable, balanced and business-like, or else the other party may challenge it whenever it wants to get rid of the promised exclusivity.

Non-compete Clause

1. A non-compete clause is an undertaking by one or more parties not to enter into or start a similar trade, business or profession against another party (or parties).

   The most common incidence is found in employment contracts, wherein an employee is required to devote his/her full time to the subject employment and not engage in another competitive venture.

Incorporate a suitable non-compete clause in your contract, if appropriate and required.

2. The reason behind insisting on such a clause is an apprehension that during the existence or upon termination of the contract, a party may start a business, and gain competitive advantage by exploiting trade secrets, sensitive information (e.g., price, marketing, clients) and other confidential information of another party. The non-compete clause seeks to stop a party from doing this.

3. There is a lot of cloud around enforceability of non-compete provisions. Normally, non-compete clauses in a contract are enforceable if they are limited in timeframe, business and geographic scope and which are deemed reasonably required to protect a party's genuine business interests (e.g., confidential information). Bear these aspects in mind while drafting/negotiating.

4. Clearly define the period of non-compete obligation and provide any consideration

for that. The consideration aspect could strengthen your argument regarding the reasonability and enforceability of this provision.

5. Specify the consequences of violating the non-compete obligations clearly. Reasonable, yet deterrent enough for a party to think twice before violating.

Garden Leave Clause

1. As an extension of the non-compete concept, there is a new concept of garden leave clause requiring an employee to give a long-term notice to employer in advance of his resignation from employment and requiring the employer in exchange to pay him full remuneration during this period when he is restrained competing.

2. Under garden leave, an employee continues to receive regular emoluments during the garden leave period and in lieu thereof, is expected to honour conditions of employment (including non-compete, confidentiality, etc.) until the expiry of the notice period.

3. Garden leave can be incorporated in employment terms from the beginning/granted on employee's request (if it suits the employer) or as part of the negotiated terms of termination. Most preferred way to enforce such a provision is to specify it in the employment contract.

4. You should keep in mind that during garden leave an employee is under contract (and still bound by his/her employment terms, e.g., confidentiality). This means that if the employer changes its mind, the employee may even be asked to return to work at any point during the notice period.

5. During garden leave, an employee may be subjected to certain restrictions. e.g.:
   a. No access to particular software/ information.
   b. No invite for meetings/calls.
   c. No access to clients/vendors.
   d. No media statements about the employment/termination.
   e. Bar on professional engagement elsewhere.
6. While drafting a garden leave clause, bear in mind that it is to be used to protect the business and reputation of an employer when a very senior and key executive's employment is to be terminated. This clause is to be used sparingly for employees having great access to the employer's resources and information. Be judicious in suggesting such a clause.
7. Another reason for judicious use of the garden leave clause is that it comes at a heavy cost to the employer (without any services being rendered by the employee). A cost-benefit analysis is required.

Non-Solicitation

1. It is customary to provide this clause alongside the non-compete clause in commercial contracts. This clause is generally executed with employees or independent contractors to safeguard a party resources (employees, agents, clients, suppliers, etc.).

2. Under a non-solicitation clause, one or more parties agree that for a certain period of time (during or after expiry of the contract), they

will refrain from engaging in business that is competitive to the existing/newly acquired/ newly started business and will not try to entice or poach each other's customers or employees respectively.

3. A non-solicitation clause is very important when a company engages a high-profile professional as its employee/advisor/ consultant exposing a lot of clients/ employees to him/her or a larger company acquiring a smaller one that operates in the same industry.

4. Non-compete clause prevents a party from engaging with a competitor or from creating a competitive business to either party; whereas a non-solicitation clause bars a party from luring or hiring the employees/ clients of other party for a certain period of time. The underlying objective here is safeguarding important people and confidential information with them.

5. Contract drafting is not a theoretical subject. It is learning by doing and experiential learning subject. The more you practice and the more you work in this field and continue a quest for learning/improving, the better you will get.

6. Each section of the draft should represent well-arranged pieces of a puzzle which, if read as a whole, should provide pictorial clarity.

Default/ Breach

1. Define what actions/consequences would be considered as a default or breach under a contract. Many a times, a 'material breach' may have to be defined for more serious violations.

2. The consequences should be deterrent enough for the party to not think of committing a default/breach.

3. Provide a list of recourses that are available to an aggrieved party, if the other party commits a breach or is in default of its obligations.

4. If the alleged default/breach is not cured/addressed within the timeframe and other condition specified in the contract, then the non-defaulting party should have the option to avail other recourses.

5. Generally, the purpose of prescribing provisions for damages for breach of contract is to compensate the non-defaulting/injured party. The objective is not to make a profit out of the breach but to put a deterrent on the defaulting party.

"Great idea to solve the conflict with a water pistol fight!"

Remedies for Contractual breach: Damages

1. The parties can discuss and agree whether the damages can be predetermined/quantified (liquidated) or not. It would depend on the preference/requirements and nature of the transaction.

2. Most common damages are compensatory damages or actual damages, which cover the loss incurred by the non-breaching party. The amount determined as damages seeks

to make good with the actual loss caused by the default or breach. e.g.: Reimbursement of costs incurred or refund of advance paid by the non-defaulting party.

3. Another kind of compensatory damages could be special or consequential damages covering the loss incurred by the breach of contract due to special circumstances not ordinarily predictable. Such loss is actual and caused by the breach, although not directly. For example, damages for loss of an irreplaceable artefact.

"Wish me luck. I'm going in there and not coming out until all conflicts are resolved."

Liquidated Damages

1. Sometimes, parties predetermine the amount for damages required to be paid by the defaulting party in case of a non-compliance or breach. This is discussed and negotiated between the parties at the contract negotiation stage. The objective is not to make money out of the non-compliance but to encourage parties to be compliant.

2. This amount need not be exorbitant but should be high enough to discourage a party to even think of making a wilful default. It should outweigh the benefit a defaulting party could think in terms of pursuing an alternative opportunity.

3. Liquidated damages are not the general rule and are prescribed for rare/specific instances. You should list the instances which would trigger liquidated damages.

4. You may prescribe an amount or a ratio or formula to calculate the liquidated damages in case of a default.

5. The court may not be inclined to uphold the liquidated damages if they find the amount to be grossly excessive or in cases where the actual damages can be easily determined.

6. If the court feel the liquidated damages clause is reasonable and necessary they will not look into the actual damages suffered by the non-defaulting party.

My conflict resolution skills are sorely needed here

Specific Performance

1. In some cases, a non-breaching party may not be satisfied with damages and may seek a specific performance. Specific performance is an equitable relief to enforce contractual obligations between the parties.

2. You may incorporate suitable provisions for seeking specific performance in cases wherein monetary damages are inadequate to compensate your client's claim for a default.

"Do we see eye to eye
on this matter?"

Rescission

1. Rescission of a contract is another remedy that a non-defaulting party may resort to. When a party to a contract does not fulfil its obligations, the other party can rescind the contract and refuse the performance of its obligations.

2. The party which rescinds a contract must restore any benefits it enjoyed under the contract and/or is entitled to receive damages/compensation for any loss suffered due to such rescission.

Injunction

1. A non-defaulting party may seek a decree for specific performance against the defaulting party.
2. A court may also issue an injunction to stop a defaulting party from doing something it promised not to do under the contract.

Territory

1. Define the territory wherein the contract will operate. In the absence of such a stipulation, the parties may be at variance in their expectations.

2. Along with defining territory, specify whether the relationship between the parties is exclusive within the territory or can they do business with others.

3. Stipulate the consequences of a party trying to operate out of the territory assigned to it under the contract.

Costs

1. Some contracts entail significant costs. For example, due diligence, consultants fees, travel, samples, trials, registration, stamp duty, etc. Discuss and allocate these costs to the parties, if required.

2. Costs incurred towards a contract may be allocated among parties in one of the following ways:

a) Entire costs to be paid by one party;

b) Costs to be shared equally by all the parties;

c) Cost of specific elements be borne by specific parties.

3. Method of incurring costs and payment modalities should be provided, i.e., whether to be incurred directly by a party or to be reimbursed to the party incurring such expenditure.

Other Clauses: Indemnity

1. Invariably every contract includes an indemnity clause. This clause acts as a security or protection for an affected party against loss or other financial burden.

2. Under the indemnity clause, a party promises to compensate the other for any liability/ loss arising out of the agreement when the former is at fault.

3. You may also incorporate the formula/ methodology to calculate the amount of

compensation to be provided towards indemnity.

4. Indemnity provision virtually acts as an inter-party insurance policy fixing risk and liability between the parties. The indemnitor pays for the losses suffered by the indemnitees.

5. Sometimes, the indemnity can include not only compensation but defence too. Here the indemnitor will pay for the losses of the indemnitee and will also defend the indemnitee against any legal claims at its own cost.

6. While drafting the indemnity clause, you may limit your client's exposure to indemnify the other party only to certain types of claims or to a specific amount of loss.

7. A party may agree to indemnify the other for all liabilities or losses incurred in connection with specified events or circumstances without any specific limitations.

8. In case of limited indemnity, a party agrees to indemnify the other against losses except those incurred as a result of the latter's own acts or omissions.

Reverse Indemnity

1. Under this, a party agrees to indemnify the other against the losses incurred as a result of the latter's own acts and/or omissions.

Third party indemnity

1. A party agrees to indemnify the other against any potential liabilities to or claims by a third party.

Mutual or party to party indemnity

1. Under this, each party agrees to indemnify the other(s) for losses incurred due to the former's breach of the contract.

2. Be careful in specifying the duration of the indemnity provisions, whether the obligations will be effective during the subsistence of a contract or even after expiry or termination thereof.

3. A time limit may be prescribed for bringing about any indemnity claim by an affected party. The window should not be kept open forever.

4. Treat indemnity clause as an important fall-back option and not part of the standard terms and conditions. It is going to be the go-to option if your client is in a soup later on.

5. The indemnity clause should not be a blank cheque to the indemnitee. The affected party must take all reasonable steps to avoid/ mitigate the loss. While drafting, cast an obligation accordingly.

6. Specify the mechanism for indemnity – Notice, time period, defence in courts, payment in the nature of compensation/ reimbursement, etc.

"I will of course yield to whomever agrees with me."

Guarantee

1. A guarantee is a secondary obligation which triggers only if the primary one is not met. Draft the provisions bearing this aspect in mind.

2. Parties to a contract may insist on a guarantee clause (even a standalone agreement on the subject).

3. Ensure that in a guarantee provision, the guarantor assures the creditor/claimant that

the principal debtor should be trusted and in case of its default the guarantor shall pay up. A guarantee may thus be perceived as a back-up plan, a security given to the creditor.

4. All the three stakeholders must be on board regarding all aspects, including the extent of the guarantee - when it is triggered, exact obligation of the guarantor, limitations, qualifications, etc.

5. Since the objective of a guarantee is to secure the payment of the debt taken by the principal debtor, it triggers only if there is a valid claim. If there is no valid claim (debt becoming void, time barred, etc.) no obligation subsists for the guarantor to fulfil – demarcate this clearly in the contract.

6. Guarantee may be specific (for a single debt/obligation) or continuing (extends to a series of transactions). The contract must ensure that a guarantor's liability continues till all the transactions are completed or till the guarantor revokes the guarantee (if revocable).

7. The guarantee clause should stipulate that after making a payment and discharging the liability of the principal debtor, the guarantor will have various rights against the principal debtor, creditor, and any co-guarantors.

8. Ensure that after satisfying the guarantee towards the creditor, the guarantor steps into the shoes of the creditor and can deal with the principal debtor in that capacity, i.e., the guarantor has the right to recover the amount which she/he has paid to the creditor which may include the principal amount, interests, and other costs.

9. Create an ecosystem making sure that after paying off the debt of the principal debtor, the guarantor becomes entitled to claim all the securities provided by the principal debtor to the creditor irrespective of the fact whether the guarantor has any knowledge of those securities or not.

10. If there are several co-guarantors, in the absence of any contract to the contrary, they

should be made liable to contribute equally. This holds good even when the liability of co-guarantors is joint or several, and whether it's under the same or different contracts and whether it's with or without the knowledge of each other.

11. Ensure that if the co-guarantors agree to guarantee different sums, they contribute equally, subject to the maximum of the amount guaranteed by each of them.

12. Stipulate that a guarantor shall stand discharged from liability:

    (i) upon revocation of the guarantee,

    (ii) by conduct of the creditor, or

    (iii) by invalidation of guarantee.

13. Provide that if the creditor makes a contract with the principal debtor resulting in release of the principal debtor or there is an act or omission of the creditor which results in the discharge of the principal debtor, the guarantor too stands discharged.

14. Confirm that in the absence of a stipulation to the contrary, the guarantor's ability is co-extensive with that of the principal debtor and the former is only liable to the same extent as the latter, and nothing beyond.

"I take it he's learned karate."

Term/ Duration of Contract/ Effective Date/ Termination Date

1. Do not forget to mention the term or duration of the contract, i.e., the period for which the contract will be effective.

2. Along with the duration, mention the effective date of the contract. The term of the contract will commence on that date and the expiry date will be calculated accordingly.

3. The duration of a contract may sometimes be dependent on the completion of a specific project or a series of transactions.

4. Prefer time bound contracts as much as possible. If the parties are comfortable in a relationship, they can always extend or renew the contract.

5. Avoid a contract to be perpetual, if possible. Having to terminate it if the going is not good is a tedious exercise and creates negativity and disputes at times. An automatic expiry on completion of its term is a much better option.

6. Be very careful to observe the hidden 'automatic renewal' clause on the expiry of the contract. A party may be thinking of terminating or renegotiating at the expiry of a contract and suddenly it may receive invoice for the next term by the other party, citing the automatic renewal.

7. Renewal or extension of a contract should be a considered and a conscious decision of the parties. Incorporate a suitable mechanism to facilitate it in the contract.

8. Incorporate, *inter alia*, the timelines, notice requirement, offer and acceptance, deemed acceptance, etc., aspects in an extension/renewal clause.

9. Minutely discuss and observe all the terms and conditions (if any) that are undergoing a change in the renewed/extended term and provide sufficient clarity in that regard.

10. Take a judicious call in considering the substantial changes in the subject matter/terms and conditions of the contract in the renewed/extended term. A fresh agreement would be a better option or an extension/renewal letter or amendment agreement will do.

Representations & Warranties

1. A representation is a statement of fact made during contractual negotiations in order to induce/convince another party to enter into a contract.

2. Re-emphasising on the core difference, a representation is an inducement for a party to enter into a contract, whereas a warranty is an essence of the contract regarding a party's behaviour and performance (on the basis of representations) during the contract term.

3. Representations are usually made prior to the contract. However, more often than not, they are repeated and form an important basis for the parties to enter into a contract.

4. A warranty is a promise that particular statements made by a party are true at the date of the contract or will continue to be true for a particular period.

5. The representations pertain to past facts or existing circumstances related to the contract, which influences the decision of the other parties to enter the contract.

6. These two terms seem similar but are different. In terms of order or sequence, warranties follow representations.

7. A true and correct representation of facts is mandatory to constitute a sound contract. If a representation is found to be incorrect or untrue, it entitles the recipient of such representation to claim misrepresentation and rescind the contract itself.

8. A recipient of misrepresentation should act in a timely manner as the right to rescind the contract may not hold good forever. If the contract is affirmed, substantially acted upon or significant time passes, it may be tough to rescind the contract.

9. The most common remedy for a recipient of a warranty is to claim damages in case of breach of warranty if it results in a loss to the recipient (reasonably contemplated, not too remote).

10. The need and extent for representations and warranties depends on case-to-case basis (e.g., considering the subject matter, stakes involved, tenure of the contract, etc.).

11. If you are representing the seller, you wish to provide as less representations and warranties and for as less a period as possible. The situation reverses when you are representing the buyer side.

12. It may be a bit unreasonable to expect perpetual representations and warranties (at

least in fixed duration contracts). No one would like to live with a bottomless pit and an unknown perpetual exposure.

13. If the recipient party's remedy lies in damages, the least that would be expected is to put it in the same financial position it would have been if the breach had not occurred. Therefore, an expected level of loss occurred due to the breach should be assessed.

14. In practice, both/all parties provide representations and warranties disclosing material information in M&A and certain other contracts. Invariably, the seller's/the target's representations and warranties are more elaborate and extensive as they pertain to information about the target or business and the securities or assets/liabilities which are the subject matter of the contract.

15. In loan agreements and other finance agreements, the borrower provides representations and warranties to induce and comfort the lender to provide loans. If a representation is no longer true, the lender

retains the right to enforce its stipulated remedies against the borrower.

16. The recipient needs to believe a representation to be correct in order to enter into a contract. However, the effectiveness of a warranty will have to be tested when a representation turns out to be inaccurate in future.

"Visualize yourself not falling off the wall."

Force Majeure

1. 'Force Majeure', a nominal clause appearing towards the end of most contracts was an orphan. No one used to even read it properly, let alone know the implications or debate on it. 99% of the times, it used to be a cut and paste clause.

2. However, COVID-19 brought this clause into prominence. It is the most debated term for enforcement of contracts in the last 4 months.

Next few tips, therefore, will be centred around it.

3. Firstly, you must have a force majeure clause in your contracts depending on the subject matter (goods, services or promises) of the contract. First and foremost, you must comprehensively define what events/ circumstances will constitute 'force majeure'.

4. Force majeure refers to a clause invariably incorporated in contracts to suspend/remove liability for natural and unavoidable events/ circumstances which interrupt the normal course of a business and prevent the affected party(ies) from fulfilling obligations.

5. While demarcating the events/circumstances to be included in the scope of 'force majeure', bear in mind that there are broadly two kinds of events - natural and political. To qualify as a 'force majeure' event, it must be an uncontrollable event. Anything that the parties can anticipate, control or mitigate by any means would not qualify as force majeure.

Force Majeure Clause Exclusions

1. In addition to identifying the events which would trigger force majeure provisions, we should also be careful to specify the exclusions. Events which the parties deem certain, foreseeable or avoidable should be excluded from the scope of force majeure.

   At the end of the day, the onus rests on the party invoking the force majeure provision to demonstrate circumstances beyond its reasonable control.

2. The force majeure clause is not an escape route for your contractual obligations. This provision can be resorted to only in drastic, unforeseeable, unavoidable circumstances. Parties must take all reasonable steps to avoid/ mitigate the situation by exercising business-like care and attention. Negligence or shirking one's responsibilities are not good reasons.
3. For example, if a party does not take good care of your customer's material and let it rot in sun or rain, it can't suspend or avoid its obligations by claiming force majeure.
4. Set a tolerance level in force majeure clause.
5. If the force majeure event continues for too long, the parties should have the right to terminate the contract. You should not make them wait endlessly, and must specify a period after which they can terminate.
6. A party cannot invoke 'force majeure' clause merely because the situation has become less economically attractive or more onerous for it to perform its obligations or an available alternative course of action is less/not profitable. Impossibility of performance is the key.

Termination of Contract

1. A contract typically comes to an end when the parties' obligations or actions thereunder are completed. Therefore, the parties must keep a record of the fulfilment of their obligations or actions diligently.

2. Sometimes, the obligations of the parties or the actions under the contract may not have been completed, yet one or more parties wish to walk out of the contractual relationship.

You may have to carve out a provision for such an eventuality.

3. A contract may also come to an end on its own by efflux of time stipulated in the terms. The parties in such a case do not need to take any explicit action for the contract to come to an end.

4. Termination of a contract could be either mutually agreed by all the parties or initiated by one or more parties.

5. One of the most forceful/common grounds for termination of a contract is the non-performance of its obligations by a party. In such a case, the non-breaching party gets to seek termination.

6. For termination of a contract on account of non-performance of its obligations by a party, set clear benchmark of a default/breach or material default/breach. Mere allegations will not hold good.

7. Impossibility of performance of a contract is another reason for termination thereof.

8. At times, there are instances of a party misrepresenting facts to induce the other party to enter into a contract. Once known, the other party can rescind the contract.

9. A party seeking termination of a contract must deliver a written notice.

10. In addition to legal situations rendering a contract open to termination, the parties can also pre-agree for the eventualities wherein the contract will be terminated.

11. The termination notice clause must specify the provisions of the contract providing the right to the seeking party to terminate the contract.

12. The termination ecosystem in the contract should specify the timeline of termination (immediate effect or within a specific time) in accordance with the contractual terms.

13. Termination with immediate effect is a drastic measure and should be resorted to only in exceptional situations as afforded by the terms of a contract. Providing a reasonable time is the norm. Draft your termination clause bearing these facts in mind.

14. Sometimes the parties may resort to a termination notice/call to remedy. This is to say, asking a defaulting party to remedy a defect, else the contract shall stand terminated.

15. Parties must be careful in drafting a termination clause which allows them to terminate the contract at will (without assigning any reason) – such contracts, being determinable contracts, cannot be specifically enforced. Is it worth taking such risk?

16. Since a contract terminable at will cannot be specifically enforced, it may leave parties only with a relief in terms of an award or compensation for the notice period.

Therefore, provide suitable measure while drafting a termination clause allowing termination at will.

17. One should remember that a termination notice is not by itself equivalent to termination of a contract. Termination notice is in the nature of a warning by a party to the others that the contract will terminate - whether with immediate effect or within a stipulated time depends on the terms of the contract and notice.

18. Why termination clause?

    Among other reasons it helps in stipulating which breaches are serious enough to warrant discontinuation of a contractual relationship. Else, the parties may keep fighting and arguing whether a breach was serious/significant enough.

19. Sometimes you may like to explore/test a commercial relationship (particularly with a new party) and keep your options open to continue or discontinue the relationship,

without having to assign a reason or having to justify your decision. A termination clause allowing parties to terminate at will helps in such a case.

20. Do remember, a termination clause is not a 'Right to forget' or 'Right to absolve' clause. The parties are liable to fulfil their obligations incurred before the effective date of termination. You just cannot walk away from a contractual relationship forgetting it as a bad dream – compare it with a divorce – what happens to your kids?

21. A contract should be structured in a 'To-do' or 'Operations' manual way. Whenever in doubt about anything, an easy understandable flow, indexing, etc., will reduce parties' effort of reading the entire contract to find or refer to anything it wants.

Survival Clause

1. The survival clause in a contract stipulates as to which terms and conditions of the contract will remain in effect even after the termination or expiration of the contract.

2. Most common examples of contractual obligations covered under the survival clauses are non-compete, confidentiality, dispute resolution, and non-solicitation, to name a few.

3. The need for survival of specific clauses differs from case to case. Review the contract and parties' relationship thereunder to determine which clauses are of importance for your client to survive the expiry or termination of the contract.

4. Survival provisions should not only contain the provisions which are supposed to continue, but also the period of such survival post expiry or termination. Specify the period against each provision intended to survive.

Relationship of Parties

1. Specifying the exact nature of the relationship of the parties, e.g., independent parties, partners, principal to principal, master-servant or others, to avoid any ambiguity, particularly with respect to the respective authority/obligations of the parties.

2. Specifying the nature of the relationship of the parties helps in determining their respective rights and obligations beyond what is prescribed in the contract, if need be.

3. This clause will be key in determining the representation rights of each party to the people/parties outside the ambit of the contract on behalf of the parties e.g., an agent/distributor/licensee has the right to represent the master/licensor.

4. The relevant clause should specify if or up to what limits the parties have the right to represent each other to outsiders, leaving no scope for any misrepresentations.

5. Any misrepresentation made by or undue advantage sought/derived by a party beyond the scope of their contractual relationship must be suitably dealt with. It could also be described as a material breach of the terms.

6. Describing the exact relationship of parties is also relevant from a taxation/enforcement perspective. In certain cases, tax authorities may seek scrutiny of certain contracts to see a 'Related Party' or 'Permanent Establishment' angle for lacking genuineness of transactions and consideration.

Relationship of Parties

1. These are perceived to be non-substantive, non-important and standard clauses different from transaction specific clauses in the contract, mostly finding place in the second half or even the last quarter of a contract.
2. Most of the boiler plate clauses are inserted and agreed upon blindly without enough attention, negotiation and corrections.

Q: Is it necessary to incorporate boiler plate clauses in a contract?

A: No.

Do you want to take the risk?

Q: Are not all boiler plate clauses dull and boring?

A: Yes.

Still, do you want to take risk of not reviewing or negotiating properly and compromising your client's interest?

Q: Are not all boiler plate clauses the same?

A: Yes, but they need to be customised for each contract.

Q: Why should we bother about the boiler plate clauses when they are all the same?

A: A dispute can arise out of any word (not even a clause) in the contract, so better pay attention to each provision.

Q: These boiler plate clauses have been there for ages in all our contracts, no issue has arisen ever. Why should we waste time in reviewing and negotiating the boiler plate clauses?

A: 1. The devil lies in the details.

2. There is always a first time.

3. These clauses can/are usually deliberately drafted to benefit/deprive either of the parties. The one who is drafting it is in an advantageous position, if the other party is not diligent enough.

4. The consequences of a blind transposition of boiler plate clauses (without application of mind, review, and negotiation) can be very severe for the parties.

5. The clauses deemed ordinary or inconsequential tend to generate most business for litigation lawyers. So, start paying attention.

6. The implications of blind transposition of boiler plate clauses become apparent only when things start going wrong between the parties. Else, all can afford to sleep well.

7. Sometimes (for a change) the parties may want a short and crisp agreement without too much of legalese which they cannot understand. You should be judicious enough to determine which bare minimum boiler plate clauses should still be inserted to secure your client's interest.

Further Assurances

1. The parties need a lot of support from each other in pursuance of a contract (information, support letter, resolutions, etc.). An assurance clause mandates that each party shall execute and deliver all that is required to this effect.
2. This clause helps in making the parties more proactive and accountable in providing all requisite support for effectuating and operating a contract.

3. The underlying idea is to exert moral pressure and seek commitment from all parties to cooperate. No party should have the leverage to withhold any support at any stage.

4. This clause should be drafted with safeguards and all request for cooperation should be reasonable and need based.

5. If the requests for cooperation are not reasonable and need based, a party may feel bullied by a stronger party who has more bargaining power while drafting the contract.

6. After the initial enthusiasm, sometimes, parties start lying low and become indifferent and unresponsive. This clause keeps them in check.

Taxes

1. Contemplate which taxes could get triggered with the contractual transactions and suitably allocate the onus on the parties.
2. Mention whether the payments to be made under the contract are subject to taxes or net of taxes.
3. Check whether the (international) parties can get any tax benefit under the bilateral tax treaties.

4. Cast tax withholding and deposit responsibilities on the parties. The parties should provide suitable tax certificates to each other to take benefit in their tax returns.

No set off/ Counter Claim

1. This clause is mostly used in loan agreements to protect the lender from the borrower setting off amounts due to her/him against any amount allegedly claimed by the borrower.

2. The borrowers typically try to claim set offs and raise counter claims for delays in disbursements, etc. A no set off clause provides that the borrower shall have no such claim.

3. All said and done, this clause is not an absolute protection for the lender and courts may entertain a counterclaim by the borrower on the merits of a case.

"We only have a few rules around here, but we really enforce them."

Publicity

1. Different parties have different reasons and objectives for entering into a contract. It may be a routine matter for one, and a 'trophy' transaction for another. To what extent the parties may publicise the contract and terms thereof should be agreed upon by the parties.

2. Each contract is negotiated on different parameters and some variance/exception may be agreed upon due to some special circumstances. A party may therefore be

hesitant for third parties to know particularly the commercial terms of a contract and may like to place restriction on the publicity of these terms.

3. The parties should indicate whether all or any particular term of a contract shall be subject to non-disclosure to third parties.

4. Sometimes the legal requirements of disclosure of commercial relationships may differ between parties, consequently the respective obligations may also differ.

5. The publicity clause should also incorporate exceptions to the general confidentiality provisions.

Signature

1. You may get each page of the contract initialled by the representatives of each party and signed full on the signature page.
2. The idea behind getting each page of the contract initialled by representatives of each party is to avoid any page being replaced by a party at a later stage.

3. Some law firms also have made it a practice to affix their seal/stamp on each page of the contract to minimise replacement of any pages of any party.

4. Along with the signature, the name of the signatory representing the party, designation of the signatory, date and place of execution must be mentioned.

5. For further authentication of signature, you may like to match it with the signatory's signature on any official identification issued to such person. This will minimise the possibility of signing differently and refusing the execution.

6. Some organisations are very particular and have strict rules about execution of the documents on their behalf. You should ensure that the signatory is properly authorised.

7. If an organisation has a stipulation about affixing its rubber stamp/seal on the documents, ensure it is adhered to. Leave no ground for variance and denial thereafter.

8. At times, parties may be located at different places and signing from their respective place at the same time. Device a suitable exchange of documents by e-mode so that signatures of all of them can be accommodated on each page and the signature page.

Minor Changes

1. Sometimes, there could be some minor mistakes noticed after printing of the contract or some dates may be blank. It may be corrected/filled up by someone and all parties/their representatives should authenticate it.

Number of Copies

1. How many copies of an agreement should be printed? Every party may want an original copy. If the stamp duty on the contract is high, get one original and other certified copies.

Witnesses

1. A good way to ensure for the authenticity of the execution of a contract is to have some independent persons acting as witnesses, i.e., people having no stake in the subject matter.

2. Many a times, things go wrong between parties and they deny having executed the contract in the first place. It is good to have witnesses to avoid (or at least minimise) such situation, even if it may not be legally required.

3. If a contract requires registration, the registration authorities insist on witnesses. Keep them handy.

Annexures

1. An annexure means something added or attached to a larger or more important document, an agreement in this case.

Schedules

1. It means a table, catalogue, list, etc., of minor details which, instead of being incorporated in the operative or boilerplate clauses, is enclosed separately.

Annexures/ Schedules

1. The idea of appending these to a contract is to avoid too many details in the main body of the contract that may disturb the flow thereof.

2. These enable a reader to concentrate more on the operative/boilerplate clauses of a contract rather than the ancillary information which may not be as important for everyone.

3. If a reader is interested in the details mentioned in these, he/she can straight away check the information in the concerned annexure/schedules.

4. Some common examples of information in annexures/schedules are: business plans, timelines, organisation charts, representatives and warranties.

Exhibit

1. It means reproduction of some other document, e.g., a government approval, character documents of a company, another contract.

2. In order to be legally enforceable, even e-contracts must satisfy all the requisite requirements of a contract under the Indian Contract Act, 1872 (e.g., offer, acceptance, consideration, free consent, etc.)

3. It is quite common these days for parties to communicate and agree on terms and conditions of a commercial relationship over email. This could amount to a legally enforceable agreement, i.e., a contract. However, such emails would invariably be brief and capturing only a part of the understanding of the parties as well as miss various important aspects – it is advisable to convert the email discussion into a full-fledged proper contract.

Spell Check

1. Carry a thorough spell check on a contract. A computer may not distinguish among 'to', 'two' or 'too' at times.

2. Do not rely completely on your computer for spellings and grammar, it may still miss some mistakes. Read the document thoroughly before sending to it anyone.

Readability Check

1. The very learned Otto Stockmeyer (Retired Professor, Western Michigan University Cooley Law School) suggests that in addition to spell check, you may as well run a readability check.

   There are several such checks available online to find out whether your text is easy to read.

Corresponding on a Draft

1. Never send a draft contract (or any document for that matter, which is not finalised yet and is subject to other party's feedback) in a PDF format or in a read only mode. This will lead to a waste of time in seeking/granting permissions.

Language

1. If any reader is unable to understand the contents of a contract, the one drafting it has failed in his job. One does not draft for one's own literary pleasure, but for the benefit of readers and the effective implementation of the contract.

One-sided Contracts

1. You may get carried away and draft a contact heavily loaded in your client's favour. It will certainly not be executed on the dotted line, unless the other party is desperate.

2. Drafting such contracts may lead to the breakup of discussions between parties if the other party feels humiliated and belittled.

3. Such a draft can only breed distrust and a lack of goodwill between the parties.

4. If your draft is not a balanced one, be ready for the other party's counterproposal, a new draft from their side rather than using your draft.

A Balanced Draft

1. A draft which takes care of each party's genuine concerns from the word go saves time, breeds trust and goodwill and makes the recipient of the draft contract think twice before objecting or bargaining on any issue.

Cross Referencing

1. Try to avoid cross referencing to other provisions of the contract as much as possible. In case of too many revisions to the draft, it may be tough to recall and correct everywhere.

2. Too many cross references confuse and irritate the reader who will be subjected to flip the contract every now and then to understand the final position of a provision.

3. Use automated cross referencing, if possible.

Harmony

1. A contract is an amalgam of multiple provisions. All of them should be able to work in harmony.

2. Many provisions of a contract are overlapping at times. Ensure there is no inconsistency among them and that they can withstand each other.

Timing

1. Emphasize on time being of essence for the parties in the contract. Manifest its importance to the parties.
2. Your client must have given you a deadline for a draft of the contract. In your quest for perfection and improvisation, do not forget that.

Calculating time/due dates

1. Mention any specific inclusion/exclusion of days from the notice period, etc.

2. Mention 'days' or 'business days' for the calculation of any period, as appropriate.

3. If you mention 'business days', define them because different jurisdictions may have different weekly off days and public/bank holidays, etc.

4. Typically, public holidays and bank holidays are excluded from the calculation of days, if the period is quite short.

Easy to Read

1. Divide different subject matters in small paragraphs. The endeavour should be to make it reader friendly.

Multiple contracts

1. Sometimes, multiple contracts are executed to effect a transaction. You should clarify as to which contract's provisions will prevail in case of any inconsistency between different contracts.

2. Avoid overlap and ensure consistency as much as possible in the multiple contracts executed in respect of a transaction.

Table of contents/ Index

1. If the contract exceeds 4-5 pages, an index or table of contents will enable the reader to find the relevant section of the contract without much hassle or flipping.

Page Numbering

1. Number the pages of the contract, preferably in numerals.

2. You may not include the cover page, index and annexures in page numbering. Index and annexures may be numbered in a different format (alphabetically, roman numerals, etc.).

3. You may number the pages of an annexure or exhibit separately for example A1, A2.... or E1.1, E1.2, etc.

Abolish Capital Punishment

1. Use capital letters sparingly or judiciously, for example in the Title, Section, Headings, Abbreviations, etc.

Useless/ Extra Words

1. 3 a.m. *in the morning*

   Each *and every*

   Revert *back*

   Reply *back*

   Attached *herewith*

   Find and delete redundant words.

Archaic Words

1. In the year

   In the month of

   Dates as of even date

   Period of ______ days

   Use practical words instead.

Rule and Exception Order

1. Put the general proposition first and the exception later. See examples below.

   Except Sunday, the shop is open all days.

   The shop opens daily, closed on Sundays.

Put one thing at one place only

1. Avoid repetitions. Many a times, we see the same provisions appearing at different places. The more you write on the same subject at different places, the more likely you are breeding a dispute.

Break it up

1. Avoid long sentences. Not more than 20 words in a sentence, says my friend Amitabh Sharma.

2. Break long sentences into small sentences, or in sub-clauses, if manageable. It is much easier to read and comprehend.